GLOUCESTERSHIRE
THROUGH TIME
Stephen Lambe

AMBERLEY PUBLISHING

Acknowledgements

Huge thanks to Campbell McCutcheon for use of his collection. Thanks to Howard Beard, Roger Beacham and Lynne Cleaver, Tom Cherry and Meg Wise, David Aldred and Tim Curr, whose books provided old images. *Gloucestershire: A Pocket Guide* (Helm) by Carole Chester was a particularly useful reference work.

For Gill

First published 2013

Amberley Publishing
The Hill, Stroud, Gloucestershire, GL5 4EP
www.amberley-books.com

Copyright © Stephen Lambe, 2013

The right of Stephen Lambe to be identified as the
Author of this work has been asserted in accordance with
the Copyrights, Designs and Patents Act 1988.

ISBN 978 1 4456 1722 0 (print)
ISBN 978 1 4456 1734 3 (ebook)

British Library Cataloguing in Publication Data.
A catalogue record for this book is available from the
British Library.

Typesetting by Amberley Publishing.
Printed in Great Britain.

Introduction

Most of us that reside in Gloucestershire feel privileged to live here. Few counties in the British Isles provide such variation, such beautiful and diverse scenery combined with an industrial and urban environment full of rich history. The bare bones of the facts do not even hint at what the county has to offer. It is ranked sixteenth in size of the counties of England, covering 1,220 square miles. In terms of population, however, it is twenty-fifth, with less than 900 000 residents in 2011. The ethnicity of the county is also telling, with 97 per cent of us white, although in the urban areas of Gloucester city (in particular) the proportion of Afro-Caribbean and Asian residents will be much higher. The last few years have also seen an increase in the Eastern European contingent in the county.

Gloucestershire is best known for the Cotswold Hills, which dominate the eastern and southern parts of the area. Their market towns and villages won prosperity during the heyday of the wool industry and are typified by the characteristic yellow Cotswold stone. However, the other dominating geological feature is the River Severn, which shears the county in two. On the western side lies the remarkable Royal Forest of Dean, once a huge area of ancient woodland devoted to royal hunting and latterly given over to forestry – mainly charcoal manufacture – and coal and iron mining. In the north lies a remarkable trio of settlements: the ancient county capital Gloucester, the fascinating medieval and Tudor Tewkesbury and elegant Cheltenham, a town created thanks to its fashionable spa waters during the Regency period. As well as the Severn and the Avon (which meets the Severn just below Tewkesbury) the Thames also sneaks into the county on its far eastern border, at Lechlade.

On the whole, however, Gloucestershire has always been a rural county, which gives a few problems for someone seeking to show in photographic form how it has changed over the years, as I attempt to do here. Many of the county's towns and villages have remained largely unchanged over the last century or so, which can make comparative photographs somewhat dull. I hope, however, that the old photographs I have chosen provide an interesting mix. Many of these date to the years shortly before and after the turn of the twentieth century, although there are also many from the middle years of the last millennium and, in a few cases, much more recently where specific events are covered. I am particularly indebted to Campbell McCutcheon, whose superb collection comprises the majority of the old photographs in this book. Some of these images are rarely seen, while all the modern photographs were taken specifically for this book by the author. Vigilant readers will notice that while I sometimes use the tried and tested 'comparative view' approach, with an old photograph matched with a new picture with the same view, on other occasions I have opted for a more varied selection, offering a different view of the same settlement. I hope this balance keeps the book fresh and interesting. The reader will notice that the factor that has produced most change in the county over the last 100 or so years is the arrival of the motor car and the subsequent decline of the railways. Not only are cars very prominent in many of the new photographs in this book but the consequences of their presence are also there for all to see, whether they are excessive road signage, pedestrianised areas or newly-built roads. Many features of the railway – bridges and stations in the main – are now disused or have gone completely.

Structurally, I have taken the reader on a geographic journey around the county, starting in the Forest of Dean, up into the Severn Vale and its major towns, then down through the Cotswolds to the South Gloucestershire and the eastern side of the Severn. We conclude, appropriately I think, with the various Severn Bridges that link the two parts of the county north of Bristol. Inevitably, such a wide-ranging book cannot offer more than a few pages on any given settlement, so I do hope that those with an interest in the county as a whole are satisfied by this eclectic and rather personal mix of photographs.

Stephen Lambe
April 2013

FOREST OF DEAN

Lydney

We begin our journey in Lydney, the largest of the Severnside settlements. It was very much a working town, but with an emphasis on serving the docks. It also has the only surviving railway station in the area, a decent 1½ mile yomp from the town. This pair of photographs shows the town's unusual stepped war memorial from slightly different angles. The main part of the town centre is in Hill Street and Newerne Street, down the hill from the High Street where the memorial sits.

Lydney Institute

Lydney's Buildings

Many of the fine stone buildings, mainly built in the late Victorian era, still survive in the town today. However Lydney Institute (*above*), built in 1896 and later to become part of the secondary school, was demolished in 1994. Below we see another of those buildings, Lydney town hall, still owned by the town council today. It houses some community offices, but more importantly has a fine traditional concert hall. The Beatles played here on 31 August 1962 and the author's own Summers End Festival takes place here every autumn.

Mining in the Forest of Dean I

For well over 100 years, the main industries in the Forest of Dean were coal and iron mining. The area had a unique system of mine allocation called 'free mining'. Above we see Lightmoor Colliery, one of the larger mines near Cinderford, which closed in 1940. Below is some mining machinery at Hopewell Colliery, open for visits today for those interested in life below ground.

Mining in the Forest of Dean II

Right, another evocative mining shot, this time of Flour Mill Colliery, which closed its doors in 1962. Below is the free mining monument at the Triangle in Cinderford town centre. Sculpted by Anthony Dufort, it was commissioned in 2000 by Cinderford Town Council and Cinderford Labour Party.

Flour Mills Colliery, Forest of Dean, Glos. Real Photo Series 540

Blakeney, High Street

Blakeney

Blakeney is a large village on the main A48 that runs between Gloucester and Chepstow on the eastern edge of the Forest of Dean, where the Blackpool and Soudley Brooks converge. An iron forge was situated here as early as the thirteenth century.

Other Forest of Dean Industry

Above we see the Carter's factory in Coleford. Carter's was a fruit drink manufacturer that opened in 1947 and was later bought by Beechams before being subsumed by GlaxoSmithKline. Below is the Mews in Mitcheldean. Once a brewery, it now houses various local businesses, including an auction room.

Lydbrook

Two views of the village from above. This hilly parish has reputedly the longest main street in England at 1½ miles. Very much a home of the tinplate industry, its first blast forge dates back to 1608 and at the height of the Industrial Revolution it was considered comparable to Sheffield.

The Point Plump Hill, Cinderford

3731

Plump Hill

Climbing up from Mitcheldean towards Coleford, Plump Hill offers some superb views over the forest. The main difference between the new and old photographs here are obvious, even though the views are not directly comparable. The upper photograph shows the landscape dotted with the signs of industrial activity. The new photograph below shows no such thing.

Market Place, Coleford

Coleford was more able to adapt to life after coal mining, as its location in the centre of the Forest of Dean makes it an ideal base for exploration and leisure. The famous clock tower once stood with a church. However, the church proved too small for the town's growing population, and it was pulled down in 1882.

Coleford Station

Coleford actually had two stations. The one shown above is part of the Severn & Wye Railway that linked Sharpness Docks with Coleford, Cinderford and Lydbrook. The museum (*below*) now houses the junction box from the station. The Parkend to Lydney part of the line has now been restored as the popular Dean Forest Railway.

Leisure in the Forest of Dean
There are many centres of camping and caravanning in the Forest of Dean. Above we see a shot, probably from the 1960s, of Berry Hill near Coleford – birthplace of the playwright Dennis Potter. Below is a contemporary view of Whitemead Forest Park, 4 miles from Lydney.

Speech House

Lying at the centre of the Forest of Dean and built towards the end of the seventeenth century, the Speech House was the administrative centre of the forest, providing a sort of parliament for the verderers and free miners in the forest. By the 1840s it was being used as an inn, and it is now a characterful chain hotel.

Triangle, Cinderford

Cindeford was at the heart of the Forest of Dean mining industry and suffered most when mining declined between the wars. The Triangle is much changed, and its central modern development, built in the 1990s, continually divides visitors and residents. The area is now being reassessed once more for regeneration as part of the National Coalfields Programme.

Market Street, Cinderford

Both views look down Market Street away from the Triangle. It remains Cindeford's most vibrant street.

Newent

Although it sits on the northern edge of the Forest of Dean, with its half-timbered houses the market town of Newent's character is very different from the other forest settlements. Famous residents include fabled record producer Joe Meek. It is also home to the famous Onion Fayre, a one-day food and drink festival.

Old Market Hall, Newent
Built in 1668, the town's best-known building is the Old Market Hall, still used for markets today.

The Clock Tower, Newnham, Glos.

Newnham

One of the most charming villages in the Forest of Dean area, Newnham also sits on the Severn, and it is also the first site that the famous Severn Bore can be viewed. The beauty of its buildings dates back to its development as a port in the eighteenth century, though it declined in the Victorian era when the Gloucester & Sharpness Canal opened.

TEWKESBURY, CHELTENHAM & GLOUCESTER CITY

Tewkesbury I

The first three pages of our Tewkesbury section offer modern views that evoke history. One of the most important towns in Gloucestershire in medieval times, Tewkesbury is perfectly situated just above the meeting place of the Severn and Avon rivers. Above we see King John's Cottages, near King John's Bridge, which has crossed the Avon (and the man-made Mill Avon next to it) since medieval times. They are viewed from Gloucestershire's oldest pub, the Black Bear, dating from 1308. Below we see some of the quirky contrasts to be found in the town's high street: the neoclassical frontage of the somewhat older corn hall next to the half-timbered façade of Lloyds Bank.

Tewkesbury II

Two more historic scenes from very different eras. Above we see the medieval half-timbered Abbey Bank Cottages, built at the height of the abbey's power before the dissolution. Below is Healings Mill, further up the Mill Avon, which became the largest mill building in the town in the nineteenth century. It closed as recently as 2006.

Tewkesbury III
Half-timbered buildings in Church Street and a view up the Mill Avon towards King John's Bridge, showing the main drag of the Avon running parallel.

Flooding in Tewkesbury I

Our final three pages show how Tewkesbury was affected by flooding in 2007 and contrast the author's own photographs from July of that year with brand-new views of the same scenes. This first pair shows Abbey Mill. For many years this was the most important mill in town. Despite the flood defences built next to it, it tends to be the first part of the town to flood, as it did in early 2013. The building is now converted to residential dwellings.

Flooding in Tewkesbury II

This pair of photographs contrasts cyclists a few days after the rains of July 2007 in a somewhat tranquil scene with a normal busy afternoon in more recent times. Many shopkeepers were kept out of their premises for months, and a few never reopened.

Flooding in Tewkesbury III

This final pair shows flooding by St John's Bridge looking towards the garden of the Black Bear pub. Once again the height of the water contrasts with the normal scene shown below.

Queen's Hotel, Cheltenham I

Built in 1838 when Cheltenham was already established as a spa town, Queen's Hotel is one of the grandest buildings of its type outside London. It sits at the top of the Promenade, just below Montpellier. Residents have included Margaret Thatcher, Dame Nellie Melba and Sarah Bernhardt. The modern picture shows that the two cannon outside the hotel have now gone.

Winter Gardens, Cheltenham

Many of the grander parts of the town, built from the Regency to early Victorian eras, remain intact. However, a visitor from the early part of the twentieth century would notice a major omission – the Winter Gardens, the town's Crystal Palace, which was demolished during the Second World War, having fallen into disrepair. The picture above shows a gymnastics competition from 1938, and below we see the Imperial Gardens where the Winter Gardens once stood.

Lloyds Bank, Cheltenham

Built in a neo-Baroque style by Waller & Sons for Lloyds Bank, this striking building retains its power today as it did in the picture above taken in 1917, long before the High Street was pedestrianised.

High Street, Cheltenham

It is perhaps not a scene for the architectural purists, but this pair of photographs (the upper one dating from about 1925) demonstrates how the Regency buildings have been integrated almost seamlessly into the High Street. The Cotswold Pharmacy is now the laser eye clinic, while the Royal Hotel next to it has gone, replaced by the Beechwood Shopping Centre.

Everyman Theatre, Cheltenham
The Everyman is probably the finest
theatre in Gloucestershire. It was opened
in 1891 (by Lillie Langtry no less) as the
Opera House. It was renamed in 1960
and recently refurbished once again. The
modern section of the current façade dates
back to the 1980s.

Promenade, Cheltenham

This is the narrow entrance to the Promenade from the High Street. It was previously called the Colonnades. The photograph above shows the grand redevelopment on the left from the late Victorian era, which remains largely the same. The buildings to the right are clearly much more recent. Those policemen couldn't get away with standing in the road now!

Montpellier Recruiting Parade, Cheltenham, 1915
The central islands in the road shown in the lower picture did not exist in 1915, allowing the parade a clear run. The parade, held over Easter 1915, was not particularly successful, and conscription was introduced the following year.

Lansdown Fountain, Lansdown Road

The fountain in the picture above was designed and carved by ecclesiastical sculpture A. B. Wall and was moved to Sandford Park in 1929. The junction is now a busy one and the site is now a somewhat unsightly Texaco petrol station. The picture below shows where the fountain itself would have been.

Bishop's Cleeve

From sleepy agricultural North Gloucestershire village in the 1930s (*shown above*) to the centre of a large array of housing estates, Bishop's Cleeve is now served by a vibrant village centre and a large branch of Tesco. Relics of the past do still exist, though, with the thatched Kings Head pub a good example (*below*).

Gloucester Rugby Club

Gloucestershire is a Rugby Union county, and many fans support Gloucester, based at Kingsholm to the north of the city centre (*below*). Playing in the Aviva Premiership, the club has a long and illustrious history, having formed in 1873 after a meeting at the Spread Eagle Hotel. The picture above shows the team in 1912.

King's Square, Gloucester

This major shopping square in the middle of Gloucester city was still looking vibrant in the 1950s when the photograph above was taken. It has now seen better days (*below*), the victim of haphazard development and a change in shopping habits. A plan for redevelopment is in the works.

Southgate Street, Gloucester

The four 'gates' in Gloucester are now pedestrianised, but the picture above shows Southgate Street in 1905, with a tram moving through the picture. Below we see the street as it is now on a busy shopping day. The city's rich history means that half-timbered buildings rub shoulders with modern buildings throughout the city centre.

City Centre, Gloucester

Above, another wonderful view of the city centre from around 1905 contrasts with a similar view taken recently, below. Gloucester has been as affected by the recession of the last few years as any city in the county. It has been a settlement of prominence in England since Roman times, when the city of Glevum was founded during the reign of Nerva.

Bishopstone Road, Tredworth

The old photograph above gives a good impression of the uniformity of a street around the turn of the twentieth century. The stillness of the scene makes it slightly creepy – to the author at least! The modern picture shows the subtle changes that make a street such as this different today. The bare brick walls have been re-pointed in some cases, and UPVC windows have replaced the originals. The wall at the end of the street has been supplanted by a new housing development.

43

Gloucester

The previous pages show the view from Robinswood Hill on the outskirts of Gloucester contrasted with (*inset*) the same view from 1905. The Robinswood Hill County Park is run by Gloucester City Council. On this page we see Gloucester Cathedral in a 'picture postcard' view from 100 years ago compared with a recent view, complete with scaffolding. The current structure dates from the fourteenth century, although an abbey was founded on the site in the seventh century. The cloisters have famously been filmed as part of Hogwarts in the *Harry Potter* films.

Sandhurst Road, Gloucester

This elegant street is in the northern part of the city, near Kingsholm. These fine Victorian semi-detached houses have had some cosmetic adjustment over the years but still retain their character. The road actually travels all the way to the village of Sandhurst itself, a couple of miles due north of the city.

Gloucester Docks

Granted port status by Queen Elizabeth I in 1580, no other seaport is further inland in England. The Victorian development of the docks produced the array of warehouses that can now be seen there, shown both above and below. Recent regeneration has resulted in the Gloucester Quays development but has also seen the improvement and regeneration of the whole area, with the Waterways Museum prominent in keeping the heritage of the docks alive.

Pillar & Lucy House, Gloucester Docks

This pair of semi-detached warehouses (*below*) has been refurbished as part of the £40 million docks redevelopment. They sit at the northern end of the quay. Originally they stored corn and would have been next to the docks' timber yards. The original Pillar Warehouse is shown above.

Gloucester Dock and Quays

One last atmospheric shot of the docks themselves, contrasted with the retail premises still being constructed behind the warehouses. At the time of writing, most of the retailers were yet to open and much building work was in evidence.

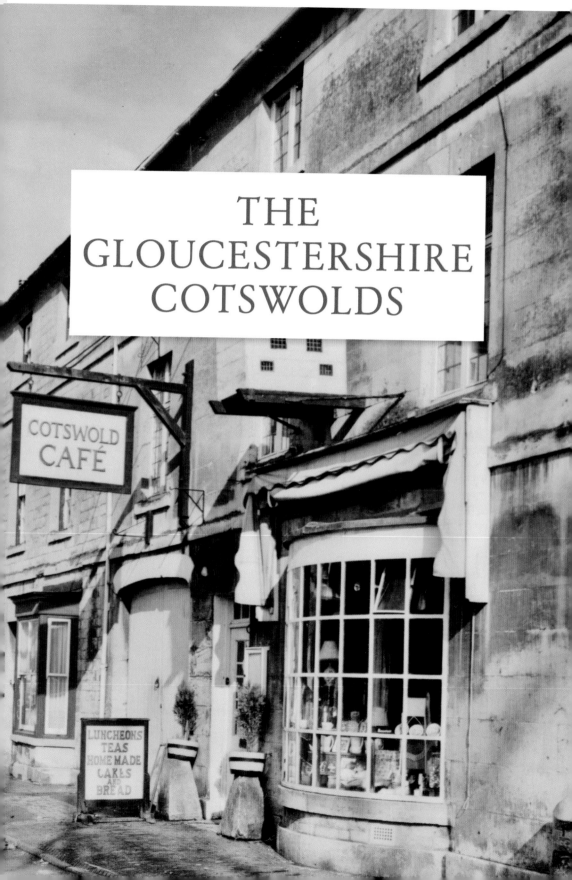

THE GLOUCESTERSHIRE COTSWOLDS

Almshouses and Church, Chipping Campden

Chipping Campden

The Cotwolds as an area is most associated with the honey-coloured limestone from which so many of its buildings are made. This gives its towns – particularly those to the north and centre of the county – a charming uniformity. Combine that with the industry that gave many of these towns their prosperity – the production of highly-prized Cotswold wool – and it is hardly surprising that these towns are so popular with visitors. This is typified by the most northerly of the Gloucestershire Cotswold towns, Chipping Campden, with its elegant terraced main street.

Moreton-in-Marsh

Set in a relatively flat patch of land on the Fosse Way, Moreton-in-Marsh has a wide main street with some typically fine architecture. It is not without its quirks, however, as the faintly eccentric sixteenth-century buildings on Curfew Corner demonstrate.

Stow-on-the-Wold I

If any town typifies the 'Cotswold experience' it is Stow, further down the Fosse Way, with its array of shops and hotels. Not built for the motor car, the hordes of tourists that visit – and park in – the town make it feel cramped on a sunny weekend day. Its location, at a confluence of major roads for hundreds of years, is what has made it so popular. This pair of photographs, with the war memorial centre stage, demonstrates how little Stow has changed over the years.

Stow-on-the-Wold II

Stow still retains a charm that all the tourists in the world cannot shake. The town was best known for its two five-day fairs in May and October, when livestock (especially sheep) would change hands in huge numbers. These still take place at a location away from the town centre, with the sale of horses now the main activity, although not completely without controversy.

Northleach

As sleepy as Stow is busy, the charming wool town of Northleach was once as prosperous as any in the Cotswolds, with a large church, dedicated to St Peter and St Paul, as a result. It lies off the A40, between Burford and Cheltenham, which has bypassed the town since the 1980s.

Fairford

Diverting east for a moment, we first come across the small town of Fairford, which lies on the River Coln. It is dominated by its parish church of St Mary, which can be seen from all round the town, as these two pictures show. In the twentieth century the town became better known for its US airbase at RAF Fairford and for the air show hosted there every summer.

Burford Street, Lechlade.

Lechlade I

Unlike in the rest of the Cotswolds, it is architecture from the Georgian era that dominates Lechlade, although Burford Street, shown in both these views, mixes old and new styles seamlessly and with some elegance.

CHURCH OF ST. LAURENCE & VICARAGE, LECHLADE.

Lechlade II

As well as having a typically fine church in the square (*above*), Lechlade is also best known as the point where the Coln and the Leach enter the Thames. The view from St John's Bridge over the Thames is fairly typical of the river above Oxford, although in the heyday of the Thames & Severn Canal the scene would have been much more industrial here, with dozens of barges moored at peak times.

Cotswold Rivers

Two river scenes. Above we see the Windrush as it snakes quietly through Bourton-on-the-Water. Rising north of Guiting Power, the river moves on into Oxfordshire, travelling through Burford and Witney before meeting the River Thames. The second shows the Coln in Fairford, which never leaves Gloucestershire, rising near Cheltenham then travelling via Bibury and Fairford into the Thames at Lechlade.

GOD SPEED THE PLOUGH
The Politician talks and talks.
The Farmer plays his part.
The Workers 25ʳ per week
Is enough to break his heart.

Cotswold Scenes
The two old photographs show scenes unlikely to be repeated today. Above, a satirical float from Fairford Carnival in 1923 bemoans the lot of the farmhand. Nothing has changed there, then! Below we see a variety of horse-drawn and man-powered vehicles outside the smithy at Coaley, near Cam.

Dyer Street Looking Towards Market Place, Cirencester

These two comparative photographs show that while the shops may have changed hands, the town itself remains unaltered. There even seem to be more cars in the upper picture! Cirencester, with is important Roman history, has been long be christened 'the capital of the Cotswolds', and it remains a thriving market town to this day, with both Roman remains and the ruins of the former abbey – demolished during the Dissolution of the Monasteries – to look at. The current church dominates most views of the town.

Cirencester
Both the River Churn and the Daglingworth Stream ran through the town at one point, and the town has been prone to flooding, as shown right. The picture below shows the finest row of shops in the Market Square, with their picturesque awnings and Victorian appearance.

War Weapons Week, Cirencester, 1941
With equipment stocks severely depleted
and invasion (supposedly) imminent,
May 1941 saw War Weapons Week, a
campaign to encourage citizens to save
using government schemes such as
War Bonds. It coincided with a series of
parades and exhibitions. In both these
pictures we see how the parades imposed
themselves on Cirencester.

Winchcombe I

The charming Cotswold town of Winchcombe, a few miles north of Cheltenham, remains little changed on the surface, although the volume of its visitors do depend on the current fortunes of nearby Sudeley Castle. Nonetheless, it remains full of character, as these comparative pictures of Gloucester Street show.

Winchcombe II

In some towns the war memorial might have been moved, but deft traffic management in Winchcombe means that it has stayed where it is. The much photographed row of almshouses was actually built for Emma Dent of Sudeley Castle by Victorian architect George Gilbert Scott.

Tetbury I

Tetbury remains one of the larger and better-kept of the Cotswold wool towns and has a pleasing grandiosity about it. Long Street is still much the same as it has always been.

Tetbury II

Two more Tetbury landmarks: Chipping Steps, which was traditionally the site of the local mop fair where farmhands would offer themselves for work, and the beautifully restored market hall at the bottom of Long Street.

Uley

Uley is a charming traditional clothiers' village, 3½ miles from Dursley. The picture above looks up the street looking towards St Giles church, while further down the hill (*below*) is a typically charming example of the village store, so rarely seen these days.

Dursley

Dursley is glimpsed in the distance in both these comparative photographs, which show the town from Woodmancote. The basic road layout remains the same, but the surrounding scene has changed considerably since the upper photograph was taken in the 1930s. The town itself mixes modern development with some lovely old buildings, including a fine market hall.

Wotton-under-Edge

Wotton is another charming wool town, but with a good silk industry as well. Its High Street offers stunning views down the hill away from the town and some well-kept shops, mixing brick and half-timbered styles.

Stroud

This is Rowcroft looking towards the junction with Russell Street. Architecturally little seems to have changed, although the motor car seems to have replaced the pedestrian these days! The statue – of George Holloway, Conservative MP for Stroud in the late Victorian era – still remains, on the right of both pictures.

Stroud Hills

The town of Stroud, which was an important cloth producer in the industrial age, exists on the confluence of five valleys. As a result it is one of the hilliest towns in the county. Here we see two hill views. The first is an old image of the Uplands area of the town, towards Slad. The modern image was taken from the Amberley office at The Hill, above Merrywalks, looking towards the Paganhill area of the town.

Minchinhampton

A tiny town rather than a village, Minchinhampton was granted its charter as a market town in the thirteenth century. It is best known for weaving. It perches on a hilltop above the Nailsworth and Golden Valleys. Minchinhampton Common is owned by the National Trust and is one of the last remaining commons in the county.

Two Stroud Area Scenes

Tom Long's post stands with pride of place at the meeting of five roads on the Common. Tom Long was supposedly a notorious highwayman, who was hung at the spot that the marker now sits. Although his myth seems not to be true, he does have a beer named after him, brewed by the Stroud Brewery. Below is a view of the Slad Valley, made famous by author Laurie Lee in his book *Cider With Rosie*.

Brimscombe

Here we see the village itself, which links to Thrupp along the Frome Valley. The older picture shows the Thames & Severn Canal in all its glory, while the lower picture shows the village as it now looks, on the hill that rises up towards Minchinhampton Common.

Brimscombe Port

This was a vital hub in the Thames & Severn Canal, as it was where cargo was transferred from the Severn Trows – the boats that carried goods from the River Severn down the Stoudwater Navigation. Beyond the port, the locks were too narrow to accommodate the trows. The port also housed several boatbuilders and some very fine offices, shown above. These buildings no longer exist, but Brimscombe Mill does, now converted to offices.

Chalford

Further east along the Thames & Severn Canal in the Frome Valley we see this view of the lock at Chalford. Below the village, by the canal are relics of the lock and the pound just below it, seen in the lower image.

Nailsworth

Four miles south of Stroud on the A46 is Nailsworth. It is impossible not to spot the Egypt Mill, next to the main road as you enter the town. It is now a restaurant and pub, but with genuine links to its heritage and two working waterwheels. These pictures, however, shows the mini-roundabout in the centre of town, which demonstrates how a street scene can change in 100 years.

THE NAILSWORTH "W"

Above Nailsworth

Another demonstration of how hilly this part of Gloucestershire is. Above we see the famous 'Ws' – the sharp hairpin bends that wind down from Minchinhampton Common to Nailsworth. Below we see Nailsworth itself, photographed, somewhat precariously, from the 'Ws'.

Stonehouse

Despite its proximity to the Stroudwater Navigation, Stonehouse is better known for its railway communications, and of course, its closeness to the M5 motorway. The town's architecture was always eclectic, as is shown in the picture above, which dates from from the 1920s. The small, half-timbered structure shown in both pictures in now a takeaway restaurant.

Painswick Stocks

The charming Cotswold town of Painswick has some lovely quirks. The town stocks, hidden round the back of the churchyard, are one of them. This superb older picture shows an expressive young urchin posing in the stocks, and they can still be seen there today, if you can fight your way past the cars.

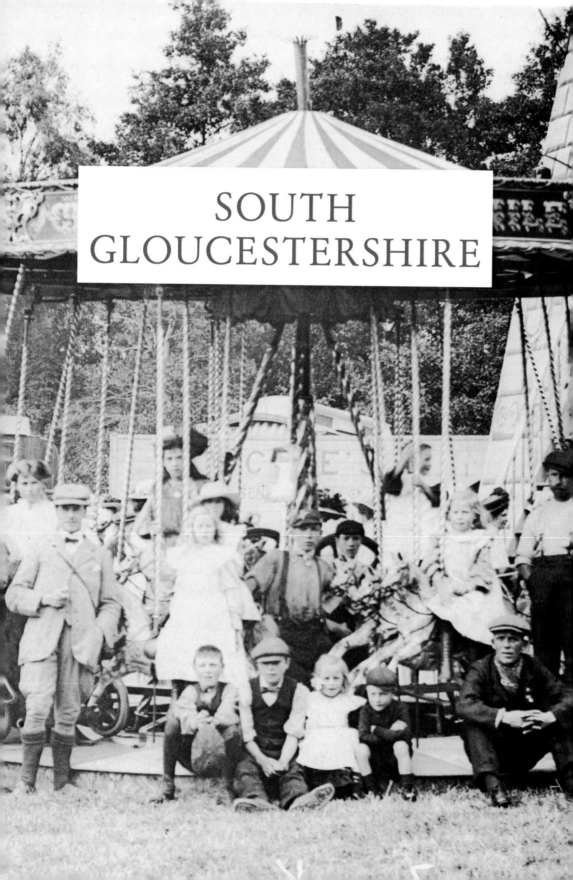

SOUTH GLOUCESTERSHIRE

Thornbury

South Gloucestershire has an entirely different character to the rest of the county, as typified by the pleasant market town of Thornbury. The town centre itself mixes styles, but is mainly comprised of relatively modern buildings, as shown here.

Thornbury

Two more views of the town. Above, the High Street is pictured 100 years ago, while below we see the town's most architecturally interesting street, Castle Street, photographed from the ornate town pump with its ironwork 'To Gloucester' sign.

The Docks, Sharpness.

Sharpness Docks

The docks began life as a simple basin giving access to the Gloucester &Sharpness Canal, which ran between Gloucester and Sharpness, mainly parallel to the River Severn. The building of a floating dock in 1874 allowed the dock to become a tidal basin and improved access to the canal by allowing a constant water level, which in turn encouraged the building of wharves and warehouses. It is still a working but somewhat quiet dock today; a visit to the site is something of an eerie experience.

Framilode, The Canal Bridge (open)

Framilode and Frampton-upon-Severn

Most of the villages close to the Severn on the eastern side have some direct connection to the river, in the form of a tributary or one of its canals. Below, horses cross the Gloucester & Sharpness Canal at Frampton, while above we see where the Stroudwater Navigation drains into the Severn at Framilode.

Cotswold Canals Trust

Saul

Above we see the old village stores at Saul next to some splendid Victorian terraces. Below is the Gloucester & Sharpness Canal at Saul Junction.

The Sodburys

The settlements of Chipping Sodbury, Old Sodbury and Little Sodbury lie within a few miles of each other in southern Gloucestershire, although the modern development of Yate has all but overwhelmed them in terms of population. Above we see the charming Cross Hands Hotel in Old Sodbury, while below is an example of the splendid Victorian architecture to be found along Chipping Sodbury's famous Broad Street.

Berkeley

Just south of Sharpness lies Berkeley, a very important settlement in medieval times. The atmospheric castle is where the imprisoned Edward II was murdered in 1327. More colourful descriptions of his death are believed to be apocryphal. Below is an example of the architecture in the unassuming town itself.

Severn Beaches

Severn Beach is in the mouth of the Severn and now lies almost under the Second Severn Bridge. The picture above shows it to have been quite a fashionable resort in the 1920s, though one suspects not the warmest. Below we see the bank of the Severn by the other bridge at Aust, with the Second Bridge in the distance. While there is a semblance of a shingle beach, one suspects it has not seen a human being for some years.

Severn Crossings

Given the importance of the River Severn to Gloucestershire life and industry, we close this book with four pages on river crossings of various descriptions. We begin with two views of the old Severn Railway Bridge. It was built in 1870 between Lydney and Sharpness to transport coal from the Forest of Dean. Damaged by barges in 1960, it was demolished in 1970.

The Severn Bridge from the Station.

The First Severn Bridge

This bridge was opened by the Queen in 1966 and was Grade I listed in 1999. It links Aust in South Gloucestershire with Chepstow in Gwent. The first of these two recent photographs shows an arch close-up and also demonstrates that pedestrians can walk the bridge should they wish, though one suspects that few do. Below is the toll station just before the bridge. Pedestrians can walk across this too, to the services on the other side of the motorway.

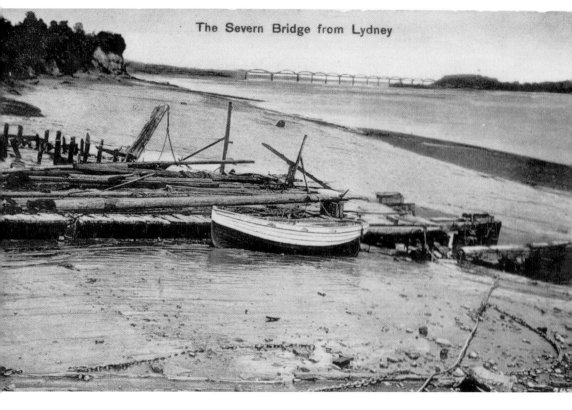

The Severn Bridge from Lydney

Severn Crossings

Above is an evocative shot of the railway bridge taken from a beach near Lydney, while below is the tiny Beachley car ferry. The Second Road Bridge made the ferry redundant.

THE FERRY, BEACHLEY.

Raphael Tuck & Sons
London.

Severn Road Bridges

Above we see the Second Road Bridge, opened in 1996 and marking the point where the river becomes an estuary. The photograph was taken from its older brother. We close with a 1960s postcard of that older brother. Note the family looking on with wonder – what a day out that must have been!

The New SEVERN BRIDGE

Index